WHY AM I. . . ?

by

CHARLOTTE MIZE

Copyright 1989
Charlotte Mize
Colorado Springs, CO

2809 Granny White Pike
Nashville, TN 37204

DEDICATION

To Eddie, my son, who taught me how to use a computer and refrained from laughing at my ignorance.

To Bob, my husband, and to my other children who at times may have felt neglected as I worked on these lessons.

To the women who graciously allowed me to teach the principles found in these lessons and were encouraging to me.

FROM THE AUTHOR

There is a great resurgence among Christian women of the desire to study God's word for themselves. These women do not want "fluff" nor "shelled corn." By fluff, I mean busywork-type lessons that just repeat old cliches but never really touch human lives. Shelled corn lessons are those where the author has done all the study and tells the student what to think based on the author's conclusions.

I see women who want to look into God's word to find concrete answers to real-life questions. Sometimes they feel a need for guidance in this search, but they want to make the quest their own and to base final conclusions on their own study.

This study book is an attempt to provide that kind of guidance for their search. It allows each student to find her own answers. It also encourages group discussions of common dilemmas.

May God bless you as you open his word and allow him to mold your life into his image.

Charlotte Mize

A NOTE TO TEACHERS/DISCUSSION LEADERS

This book is designed for class discussion which has been preceded by individual study of each lesson. Because many group discussions are now 90 minutes or more in length, there is much material in each lesson. If your format is a shorter time frame, encourage each member of your class/group to study the entire lesson at home the week prior to class. Then during the class time, you as a leader can determine which questions best cover the material for your group and discuss those, knowing that those in your class will have been exposed to the full scope of the lesson in their private studies.

Another suggestion for your class members might be that they study part of a lesson each day rather than the entire section in one sitting. That will encourage daily Bible study and will make comprehension easier.

TABLE OF CONTENTS

WHY AM I...

	Page
... IN THE PITS?	3
... FACING A CHANGE?	11
... OUT IN FRONT?	19
... SO BLESSED?	27
... MAKING ANOTHER DECISION?	33
... EMPTY?	41
... TOO BUSY?	49
... SURROUNDED BY CONFLICT?	59
... OFF BALANCE?	67
... AFRAID TO BE MYSELF?	73
... FORGOTTEN?	83
... HOMESICK?	91
... UNCERTAIN?	97

CHAPTER 1

WHY AM I IN THE PITS?

CHAPTER 1

... IN THE PITS?

An idealistic, totally unrealistic, picture of the Christian life is too often presented. Many expect that when one becomes a disciple, then life will always be joyous, any problems will be eliminated, and a sweet Christian spirit will win over any adversary. One may expect no tears, no illnesses, no conflicts, no heartaches. Life will be happiness, peace, light, perfect union with God. That is a picture of heaven, but not of the present age. Sin entered this world through Satan's successful temptation of Adam and Eve and with the sin came consequences. Death, illness, conflict, heartaches, and worry are all part of the continuing results of a sinful world.

Christians are surprised to find themselves in various "pits" in spite of their dedication and earnest efforts to live according to God's will. These "pits" come in many forms and spring from a variety of sources. Some are a direct result of sin or misjudgment. Others are caused by forces beyond one's control.

I. **IS THERE REALLY A PIT?**

Have you ever felt like you were "in the pits" due to circumstances in your life?

Often Christians deny these feelings. There are several reasons why.

A. *It's not "spiritual."* The reasoning goes something like this: If I trust God, he's not going to let bad things happen to me. Or, if Satan should cause problems in my life, God will show me the "spiritual" way to react.

B. *It shows a lack of faith.* Again, false reasoning comes into play: If I admit to having problems, I'm saying my faith is weak. If I had a strong faith, I would not be bothered by my circumstances.

C. *A martyr complex validates faith.* Often a person will convince himself that he is being persecuted with these problems **because** of his faith. Somehow that seems to make him feel more spiritual.

D. *Problems create a sense of failure.* Modern society has taught that successful people do not have any difficulty that they cannot handle with aplomb. Admitting an inability to cope is an admission of weakness and, therefore, of failure.

1. Do you agree or disagree with the reasoning in the four previous statements? Why?

2. Can you think of other causes for Christians to deny being "in the pits" (having problems)?

3. Is it easy or hard for you to admit you are having a problem? Why? *Fear of Independence*

Recently a series of TV ads began with the phrase, "What's a nice girl like you doing in a place like this?" That is exactly the reaction many Christians have when bad circumstances cause them to feel "in the pits."

II. WHAT PIT ARE YOU IN?

A. *Negative circumstances can affect us.*

1. Make a list of all the negative circumstances that can affect a person.

   Example: Poor health; Family tensions

   _____   _____

   _____   _____

   _____   _____

2. Which ones of the above list currently affect you? *Family*

B. *"Surely, this isn't God's will."*

The whole area of human suffering cannot be covered in this format. Many good books are available for further reading on the topic. However, for this study a brief discussion of why people face the bad times is needed.

It may **not** be God's perfect will for some things to happen. Many problems are the result of **natural consequences** of breaking the laws of nature or of sinning. The natural world works in an orderly fashion. Disruptions in that system will bring on predictable reactions. Also, God's law is systematic and irrefutable. Breaking it will likewise bring about negative responses.

Other times, God's will is being carried out through these difficult times. It may be for an individual's refinement or for furtherance of a larger plan of God (as will be seen through the lives of some Bible characters later in this lesson).

In either case, the response must be one of learning and growing. You can learn to deal with the circumstances of your life, no matter what they may be, and in the process grow from the experience.

1. What are some negative circumstances that are caused by breaking the natural laws?

    Example: Defying gravity causes broken bones.
    Unhealthy eating causes physical illness.

    risky behaviors

2. What are some examples of problems caused by breaking God's laws?

    Civil law - hiding our light

3. What problems can be caused to a person by his own personal sins?

    Falling away from God's law

4. What problems are caused by another person's sins?

5. Read Isaiah 48:10 and I Peter 1:6, 7. How does God use affliction for one's growth?

C. Read Esther 4:13, 14.

1. Was Esther in a good situation at this time?

2. Why was she there?

3. How can God's will be carried out through negative circumstances?

D. Read Luke 22:32. What is one positive result of a negative circumstance?

III. GOD'S PEOPLE WHO WERE IN A PIT

A. Joseph (Genesis 37).

1. What do you know about Joseph?

2. Why was he put in a pit (note: this was a literal pit)?

3. Later he was found in another kind of pit (jail). Read Genesis 39:2, 21, 23. How was he able to cope with this pit?

4. Why did God allow him to endure these trials? Read Genesis 45:5-8.

5. What lessons do you think Joseph learned through these experiences?

B. Paul, the apostle, suffered through many hardships (read II Corinthians 11:23-29 for a list of his "pits.")

1. What circumstances did he face?

What didn't he face!

2. In Philippians 1:21-26, he gives a reason for enduring these things. What is it?
   Stayd for their sake

3. How did Paul use his time when he was jailed?

C. Elijah (I Kings 19). His pit was depression (verse 4).

   1. How did God respond to his needs (verses 5-8)?

   2. What was God's question and Elijah's answer (verses 9 & 10)?

   3. How did God show his power (verses 11-13)?

   Elijah was in the pit of depression because he had lost sight of God's power. After he regained a proper perspective, God gave him some jobs to do (verses 15-18), and he again became productive for the Lord. God had led him to the cave for rest and for some lessons which would strengthen him for the tasks before him.

IV. HOW DO YOU REACT TO THE PIT?

When facing a bad situation, the question should not be, "What have I done wrong?" Rather, ask, "How can I react right?"

A. Below list possible reactions to a pit.

Negative Reactions	Positive Reactions
Example: Self Pity	Patience
_____	_____
_____	_____
_____	_____
_____	_____

B. Read II Corinthians 4:8, 9. Paraphase these verses in your own words.

_____

_____

_____

_____

C. Looking back over your own life, remember some "pits." From today's viewpoint, what good has come from those times?

D. Read aloud John 16:33. *What does this verse say to you?*

Romans 5:3, 4 in the Phillips translation reads:

This doesn't mean, of course, that we have only a hope of future joy - we can be full of joy here and now even in our trials and troubles. Taken in the right spirit these very things will give us patient endurance; this in turn will develop a mature character, and a character of this sort produces a steady hope, a hope that will never disappoint us.

CHAPTER 2

WHY AM I FACING A CHANGE?

CHAPTER 2

...FACING A CHANGE?

Change is a part of life. No living thing is static. Either one grows, or decay takes place.

One's ability to adapt to changes directly affects happiness and peace of mind. How boring existence would be without change.

However, some changes are difficult. In order to cope with them, one must find a perspective which makes sense of the confusion.

I. LIFE CHANGES

Below is a list of common categories of life changes. Beside each broad area, list the changes that might be included.

(Example: Age - appearance, role in family)

Age _—loss of stamina - loss of class - loss of interest_

Family _— loss of two of my children - loss of D in law_

Job _____

Finances _lower income - struggling with bills_

Health _depression - loss of stamina - diseases of age_

Moving _____

Other _— loss of dear friends - apathy in the church_

II. NORMALCY OF CHANGE

It is fun to play the game, "What if...?" What if no change had taken place in your life over the last five (ten, twenty) years? Where would you be? What would you be like?

A. Pick a past time in your life and describe it (five, ten, twenty years ago).

B. Would you willingly go back to the same situation now (identical in every way)? Why or why not?

C. For what changes from that time are you now glad?

D. Which do you wish had not happened?

E. What changes do you presently face? How do you feel about those?

III. DESIRABLE CHANGE

A. How does growth come? James 1:2-4 (see also Romans 5:3-5). Note: Change is often seen as "trouble" or "trial" or "temptation" - the very words used in these passages.

B. Can you see growth in yourself as a result of life changes? Relate one or more instances.

C. What changes does God promise and applaud?

1. I Peter 2:2

2. Ephesians 4:22-24

3. Philippians 3:20, 21

4. I Corinthians 15:51-54

IV. STRESS CAUSED BY CHANGE

On this page is a popular "Stress Test." This shows the amount of stress associated with various life changes. Some of the listed items are enjoyable, so many are surprised to find them listed as stressful. Any change causes an amount of stress, even desired changes.

This test is used to show an inclination to illness caused by a stress overload. However, illness does not have to follow a high stress score. My daughter once took this test in high school. That evening she told me, "I am about to get sick." Thinking she felt poorly, I asked her about symptoms of illness. "Oh, I feel okay. But I have a really high stress score." Physical bodies are weakened by stress, but this test only shows vulnerability to illness, not the inevitability of it.

HOLMES-RAHE STRESS TEST
In the past 12 months, which of these have happened to you?

EVENT	VALUE	SCORE	EVENT	VALUE	SCORE
Death of Spouse	100		Son or daughter leaving home	29	
Divorce	73		Trouble with in-laws	29	
Marital Separation	65		Outstanding personal achievement	28	
Jail Term	63		Spouse begins or starts work	26	
Close family member death	63	✓	Starting or finishing school	26	
Personal injury or illness	53	✓	Change in living conditions	25	
Marriage	50		Revision of personal habits	24	
Fired from work	47		Trouble with boss	23	
Marital reconciliation	45		Change in work hours, conditions	23	
Retirement	45	✓	Change in residence	20	
Family member's health change	44	✓	Change in schools	20	
Pregnancy	40		Change in recreational habits	19	✓
Sexual difficulties	39	✓	Change in church activities	19	✓
Addition to family	39		Change in social activities	18	✓
Business readjustment	39	✓	Mortgage or loan under $10,000	18	✓
Change in financial status	38	✓	Change in sleeping habits	16	✓
Death of close friend	37		Change in no. of family gatherings	15	✓
Change in number of marital arguments	35	✓	Change in eating habits	15	✓
Mortgage or loan over $10,000	30	✓	Vacation	13	
Foreclosure of mortgage or loan	30		Christmas season	12	
Change in work responsibilities	29		Minor violation of the law	11	
			TOTAL		

269
18
287

If your score was high (300 or more) be patient with yourself. Realize that a high stress level lowers such things as immunity, judgment, energy, etc. As far as possible do not add to the changes already occurring in your life. Changes that are not urgent should be postponed to a calmer time.

B. ***Read Ruth 1:1-7***

1. What changes occurred in the life of Naomi?

2. How did it affect Naomi (verses 20, 21)?

3. When she had time to adjust what was her attitude (2:20)?

4. What was the outcome of all these changes (4:13-17)?

V. REDUCING CHANGE STRESS

There are ways to minimize the negative stress accompanying life changes.

A. ***Spend time alone with God.***

1. Read the following passages and note the example of Jesus. Each time how did Jesus handle the stress?

    Luke 4:42

    Luke 5:16

    Luke 6:12

    Luke 9:10

    Luke 9:18

    Luke 9:28

    Luke 11:1

    Luke 21:37

    Luke 22:39, 40

2. Does time alone with God make a difference? How?

B. *Welcome change.* Each change brings exciting new opportunities even while it may cut off familiar patterns. Learn to live with anticipation for each new day.

1. What is the attitude found in Psalm 118:24?

2. In what way does James 1:2 suggest that we face change?

C. *Express negative emotions to someone close and caring.*

How did David express these feelings?

Psalm 13

Psalm 22:1,2

Psalm 23

D. *Have a long-range view of life.* Remember the quote: "This too shall pass away." Nothing remains status quo in this life. Any circumstances can be faced temporarily, and life is temporary.

How do the following passages help in having a long-range view of life?

Romans 8:18

II Corinthians 4:8, 9

E. ***Find stress relieving activities.*** In the midst of a change, it is very hard to summon the energy and allot time for exercise, hobbies, relaxation. However, during change times, these activities are vital.

   1. What activities relieve stress for you?

   2. Do you **regularly** engage in any of these?

F. ***Hold to the unchangeable.*** When you feel blown about like a dry leaf in a windstorm, or when you feel you are drifting aimlessly on the sea, you need a firm center for your life. **Eternal things do not change.** Latch onto those.

   What eternal promises are in Hebrews 13:5-8 and Isaiah 54:10?

CHAPTER 3

WHY AM I OUT IN FRONT?

CHAPTER 3

... OUT IN FRONT?

Women experience a conflict of emotions when the topic of leadership is discussed. Many women yearn for the opportunity to prove their abilities as leaders. Others deny being (or wanting to be) a leader in any way. However, currently in business, social and political realms women are urged to be assertive in leadership.

Because women of the church have such varied backgrounds, the subject of leadership for women is interpreted in a variety of ways. Those with a conservative heritage struggle with the appropriateness of assuming leadership in any area and especially in the church or home. Others see no disparity between God's plan for women and woman's role as a leader.

I. In order for you to determine your own emotional response to leadership, complete the following poll. (These answers are not to be judged "right" or "wrong." They are only presented to clarify your thinking.)

		Agree	Disagree
1.	I am a leader.		✓
2.	Those who want to be leaders are more egotistical than most people.		
3.	Leaders are born, not made.		✓
4.	Women do not need to develop leadership abilities.		
5.	Leadership usually means taking over a man's responsibility.	✓	
6.	One can be influential without being a leader.	✓	

7. Anyone who does not try to develop leadership abilities is shirking her responsibilities. ___ ✓

8. The Bible teaches that women MUST be leaders. ___ ✓

9. The Bible teaches that women CANNOT be leaders. ✓ ___

10. I want my daughter (granddaughter, other significant girl) to develop as a leader. ___ ✓

11. It is more important to teach leadership to young boys than to young girls. ✓ ___

12. Leaders have fewer temptations than followers. ___ ✓

13. Only people who are comfortable as leaders can be effective in a leadership role. ✓ ___

14. A person is either a leader or a follower, but not both. ___ ✓

15. Most women who assume leadership roles lose their femininity. ✓ ___

II. EVERYONE IS A LEADER.

A. For this study, accept the premise that everyone is a leader to some degree.

1. If you are a wife, you at least occasionally influence your husband. That is a form of leadership.

2. If you are a mother, you must be a leader to those children.

3. If you are a teacher, whether publicly or privately, whether in school or Bible class or your home, you lead those whom you teach.

4. If you are a friend to even one person, you at times lead in that relationship.

5. If you express an opinion in business, in volunteer services, in committee meetings, or even just to a neighbor, you have exerted that much leadership.

6. If any person seeks your advice, you are a leader.

7. If you are not invisible, you lead. Someone follows you sometime in some way.

B. You can be either a negative or positive leader. If you don't accept your role of leadership in an **active** way, you become a **negative** leader.

1. List every area where you are currently leading.

   _____

   _____

2. List all other areas of leadership available to you if you were willing or able to accept the role.

   _____

   _____

   _____

3. List the names of the individuals whom you lead (you will probably not be able to list **all** of these. Some you will not even realize look to your for guidelines).

   _____

   _____

4. What are negative ways to lead?

III. THE IMPORTANCE OF LEADERSHIP?

A. *Is it from God?*

Often it is hard to determine how much responsibility to accept. Satan can use one's pride to lure a person into becoming overcommitted. When this happens, Satan is able to destroy effectiveness. When opportunities are presented, a special time of prayer is necessary. Ask God if it is his will for you to do this. (In another lesson in this book, priorities are discussed. This lesson will provide further help in determining what God's will for you is in each opportunity.)

1. How does Satan appeal to your pride in this area?

2. How does over-commitment destroy effectiveness?

3. Do you pray about each opportunity to provide leadership?

B. *Reluctant leaders make excuses.*

Reluctant leaders can see themselves in the story of Moses. Although he was dedicated to God even to the point of renouncing his position and future in Pharoah's household (Hebrews 11:24-26), he tried to avoid God's calling to leadership. Read Exodus 3 and 4.

1. Verse 10 of chapter 3 states God's assignment for Moses. What was it?

2. List Moses' excuses and God's responses.

Moses' excuses	God's reply
3:11 _____	3:12 _____
3:13 _____	3:14-22 _____
4:1 _____	4:2-9 _____
4:10 _____	4:11-12 _____
4:13 _____	4:14-17 _____

3. What excuses do Christians make today? (This will be a long list.)

4. How do you think God responds? (See 4:14)

C. *God provides the power.*

Whenever God gives a task, he also provides the necessary resources and abilities. In answer to each of Moses' excuses, God gave either a promise, a power, or a person to supply any lack in Moses' ability.

1. Jeremiah was another reluctant leader. Read Jeremiah 1:4-10, 17-19. How did God empower him?

2. Daniel, along with three Hebrew companions, was asked to step out in front under very adverse conditions. How did God help them (Daniel 1:17-20)?

3. When Solomon became king, God offered him anything he wanted (II Chronicles 1:7). Because of the enormity of the task, Solomon had a special request (verse 8-10). What was it?

   How did God answer (verse 11, 12)?

4. Matthew 10:16-20 describes the warning and the promise given to the apostles as Jesus sent them into the world. What power was promised to them? (See also Matthew 28:18-20.)

5. List other Bible heroes whom God called to lead. With what special ability was each empowered?

_____

_____

_____

D. *Leaders must be followers.*

Effective leadership comes only through following Christ. Read Ephesians 5:1, 2.

1. Why is it important to be followers of Christ before becoming leaders?

2. Read I Corinthians 4:16, 17. Why was Paul able to advise them to imitate him? Can you make the statement found in verse 16?

E. *Christian leaders are needed.*

Christian leadership is vitally needed in our present society.

1. List areas in your community where Christian leadership could make a difference.

_____

_____

_____

2. In which of these areas can you exert Christian influence?

3. Are you presently doing so? If not, how will you begin?

CHAPTER 4

WHY AM I SO BLESSED?

CHAPTER 4

... SO BLESSED?

"Why me?" That is a common question, usually couched in a complaining tone. Whenever something bad happens, the first reaction often is "Why me?"

"Why me?" needs to be asked in another tone — one of awe and humility. God has blessed richly. He has given those blessings for a purpose. When one is a recipient of God's great gifts, then the response should be "Why me?" "Why am I so blessed?"

I. TAKE A BLESSING INVENTORY

    A. Spend 5-10 minutes listing every blessing you now enjoy. Perhaps you would benefit by "brainstorming" with another person. (Your list will be very long if you are honest and alert.)

    B. From the above list, select five blessings that are the **most important** to you personally.

       1. *Blessed by a loving Savior and the forgiveness of my sins*

       2. *I'm blessed with a fine Christian man for a husband & provider*

       3. *Blessed with a nice home and furnishings.*

       4. *Blessed with an ability to study and know the Will of God.*

       5. *Blessed with enough food & clothing*

II. WHY AM I SO BLESSED?

There are periods when everything in life is going well. No big problems. No real struggles. These respites are wonderful, but somehow a niggling little voice seems to whisper, "Why?"

One young Christian woman expressed her puzzlement. She related that she and her husband were happy, her children were normal, they had adequate income and no health problems. "Maybe the Lord thinks I'm not very strong because he has kept me from problems," was her reasoning.

Another mode of thinking might be, "What does God want from me?" "Is he expecting much in return?"

> **ABILITIES AND MATERIAL BLESSINGS ARE NEVER GIVEN TO US TO REMAIN WITH US OR FOR OUR OWN GLORY.**

A. *Read Exodus 35:30 - 36:2.*

1. What blessing had God given Bezalel and Oholiah?

2. How did God ask that their abilities and resources be used?

3. Notice that they were engaged in a "beautifying" service. Was this a waste of their blessing? Give reasoning for your answer.

A seemingly insignificant skill can be of great value when used in God's service. Never under estimate the value of your gift.

B. *Read Matthew 25:14-30 (parallel passage is Luke 19:12ff).*

1. Who was praised and why?

2. Who was condemned and why?

God expects the recipient of his gifts to use them in his service.

C. *Read II Corinthians 8:1-15.* The Macedonians were not rich, but they gave richly.

   1. What had God given the Macedonian Church (verse 1)?

   2. What attitude did they have (verses 2-4)?

   3. What proved their love (verse 5)?

   4. Why did Paul tell the Corinthians about the Macedonians (verses 6-8)?

   5. What is the motivation (verse 9)?

   6. Why did Paul urge the completion of this gift (verses 10-15)?

   7. How can our experiences be used to bless others (Galatians 6:1, 2 and Luke 22:31, 32)?

   8. What does I Peter 4:10 teach about our blessings?

   9. Genesis 12:2 concisely expressed the answer to "Why am I so blessed?" What is that answer?

III. USE YOUR BLESSINGS TO BLESS OTHERS.

A. The song *"There is a Sea"* by Lula Klingman Zahn beautifully develops this truth. Read or sing it aloud:

> *There is a sea which day by day*
> *Receives the rippling rills,*
> *And streams that spring from wells of God*
> *Or fall from cedared hills;*
> *But what it thus receives it gives*
> *With glad unsparing hand;*
> *A stream more wide with deeper tide*
> *Flows on to lower land.*

(continued)

There is a sea which day by day
Receives a fuller tide;
But all it store it keeps, nor gives
To shore nor sea beside;
It's Jordan's stream now turned to brine
Lies heavy as molten lead;
Its dreadful name doth e'er proclaim
That sea is waste and dead.

Which shall it be for you and me,
Who God's good gifts obtain?
Shall we accept for self alone,
Or take to give again?
For He who once was rich indeed
Laid all His glory down;
That by His grace our ransomed race
Should share His wealth and crown.

B. **Find Ways to Bless Others.**

1. Below copy on the left your five most important blessings from question I-B. On the other column write a way you can use each particular blessing to bless another.

    Blessings   **Use of Blessing**

    a. Forgiving Savior — lead soul to Christ
    b. *church* — meeting house — attend worship faithfully
    c. Christian mate — teach children to be Christian
    d. ability to teach — share my knowledge to others
    e. physical blessings — share what I have

2. What blessing are you currently neglecting to use for others?
   I need someone to tell me.

3. When and how will you begin blessing others with it?
   If I can as soon as possible.

CHAPTER 5

WHY AM I MAKING ANOTHER DECISION?

CHAPTER 5

...MAKING ANOTHER DECISION?

Decision making is hard! Yet every day, even every hour, brings choices — some unimportant, some life changing — some joyful, some heart-breaking.

This part of life cannot be avoided. Trying to postpone or by-pass decision-making causes complications that can become very entangled.

God wants men and women who can measure options with his measuring rod and follow through with confidence. How can you be certain your decisions are right? Where do you find confidence to proceed with a decision once it is made? Do you let others make your decisions or do you feel responsible to act on every choice that comes your way?

This chapter will look first at some personal attitudes toward decision making and then at some suggestions to consider.

I. SURVEY OF INDIVIDUAL DECISION MAKING

    A. Write a decision you made in the last 24 hours.

        1. List three **major** decisions you made in the past year.

            a. *try not to be upset about children's*
            b. *bad decisions*

            c. _____

        2. What is the most important decision you ever made (exclusively of your decision to follow Christ and the choice of your spouse).

3. What decision are you now facing?

B. Self-evaluation: (Circle answer)

1. Is it difficult for you to make a major decision?
   (Always)   Sometimes   Occasionally   Seldom   Never

2. Is it hard for you to stick to a decision once it is made?
   Always   Sometimes   Occasionally   (Seldom)   Never

3. Do you allow someone else to make your decisions for you whenever possible?
   (Always)   Sometimes   Occasionally   Seldom   Never

4. Do you look back after a decision is made and wonder about the outcome if you had decided differently?
   Always   (Sometimes)   Occasionally   Seldom   Never

5. Are you unhappy about decisions you have made in the past?   Always   (Sometimes)   Occasionally   Seldom   Never

6. Do you let opportunities pass while you are deciding?
   Always   (Sometimes)   Occasionally   Seldom   Never

II. SUGGESTIONS FOR THE DECISION-MAKING PROCESS.

A. **Set life priorities.** *Love God first, seek His kingdom*

This relieves the pressure of having to make too many decisions. By setting a course for one's life, many decisions are eliminated. Matthew 22:37 and 6:33 give some priorities for Christians.

1. What are some decisions that are eliminated by setting life priorities? *All worldly sinfull decisions if you seek spiritual things*
2. Briefly write out your life goals.

   get to heaven
   help others to get to heaven
   (Note: Another chapter in this book deals more fully with the priorities of a Christian life.)
   especially loved ones

3. How do your present decisions fit into those goals?
I am trying harder to put more time and effort into these goals

B. **Pray for guidance and wisdom.**

Too often this is left until the final step in decision making. It should be part of the early preparation for any decision, but especially important decisions.

1. What power is promised in James 1:5? *wisdom*
   mtt-7:7 - mk 11:24 others also
2. Does God help in making decisions (see Proverbs 3:5, 6)?
   also Jer 9:23 +24 - Thus saith the Lord
3. To whom can you turn for godly advice (give names)?
   God the Father, God the Son, & God the Holy Spirit
4. Is is possible to have too many advisors? Why? *Unless they are scriptural Christians possibility of wrong advice*
5. What criteria should be used in selecting advisors?
   Are they Christians - do they know the word of God, do they have lifes experiences, Do they exercise wisdom

C. **Set a deadline.**

Joshua demanded an immediate decision in Joshua 24:15. Often decisions are delayed until all the options have been removed. This limits the good possibilities as well as the poor choices. Another problem with delay is that other areas of life are held in limbo until the decision is made.

1. How do you feel when you are undecided? Is it helpful to your emotional being when you finally come to a decision? *there is an answer for everything in the scriptures* *To have helpful emotions personally have to pray and read God's word and look for examples how to solve the problem*

D. **Verbalize pros and cons of each alternative.**
whatever it is it must be godly and please Him.
Write down the choices and reasons for and against each possibility. However, beware that the longest list is not necessarily the best choice. Decisions should be made on the basis of the **strongest reason,** not the longest list.

1. Why is it helpful to verbalize the choices and the consequences of each choice?

E. *Be open to circumstances.*

   Paul had determined a course for his journey, but had to make some changes. Reads Acts 16:6-10.

   1. What changed his mind? How? *The Holy Spirit forbade Him - Prevented Him*
   2. How do circumstances affect decisions? *Often circumstances + desires make us make decisions with poor judgment*
   3. Are circumstances always a reliable guide? Why or why not? *No, because emotions tend to cause us to not think clearly also, anger, greed etc. -*

F. *Realize some decisions are not important.*

   Don't waste emotional energy and time on minor decisions which really don't have any effect. People are sometimes so bogged down in such things as what to wear, what color car to buy, etc., that they cannot face and deal with important lessons.

   1. What are daily unimportant decisions? How do you handle these?

G. *What do you WANT to do?*

   Somewhere over the past few centuries, people have accepted the mistaken conclusion that, "If I *want* to do it, I probably should not." This comes from a false humility. Rather, **God gives desires to motivate his people.**

   1. How does God answer the desires of his people (Psalms 37:4 and 103:5)? *By us delighting in the Lord. Gives us good things physically + spiritual food for the body and the soul.*

   The questions to ask regarding your desire are:

   a. Whom will it affect and how? *Is it lawful and it will certainly affect you both ways*
   b. Is there any reason not to do it? *Yes, if its not pleasing to God or causes disobedience and sin to enter into our lives*

III. DON'T LOOK BACK.

A. After a decision has been made, it is useless to look back. In fact, Jesus taught against such instability.

1. How is such a man described in Luke 9:62? *He is not fit for the kingdom of God.*
   In James 1:5-8? *Not asking in faith causes doubt. Don't assume your right and deserve God's grace.*

B. One of the greatest ways God shows his **confidence** in us is in letting us make decisions.

1. Look again at your response to question I-A-3. With that decision in mind, work through the "Suggestions for decision making." (This may take several days for some major decisions.) When you have completed this process, evaluate where you are with that decision.

2. **Remember that you have God's Spirit to guide you.**

① *I'm trying to be more understanding of people's spiritual mistakes.*

② *I'm going to love those who disrespectfully use me.*

③

CHAPTER 6

WHY AM I SO EMPTY?

CHAPTER 6

...SO EMPTY?

Do you sometimes find yourself with a gnawing hunger, an emptiness that is not physical? Perhaps you even tried "filling" that ache with a snack only to become stuffed, but the void remained.

How can people with busy lives, under constant time pressures, saturated with entertainment, and surrounded by people feel a void? Some turn to even more hurried schedules, others to escapism through chemical addictions or frenzied pleasure-seeking. But even those who are not that desperate have an uncomfortable awareness that something is missing; there is one need not being filled. "Good" people are not immune to the distress of emptiness. Peter calls this an "empty way of life" (NIV) or "futile" in I Peter 1:18.

The "hunger" comes from God. We are not complete until it is recognized and satisfied. Someone has said "There is a God-shaped vacuum in each of us." I agree. Only through God can it be filled.

I. CYCLE OF EMPTYING AND FILLING

Those terms are opposites. To tell someone the solution lies in his emptying himself and filling himself would seem to be ridiculous. But that is the message Christ brought.

Phil 4:8 fill up — II Pet 1:4-8

A. What is the message of each of these passages?

I Pet 5: Philippians 2:5-7 — *Let this mind be in you which was also in Christ Jesus!!*

Philippians 1:9-11. *To love one another and love, knowledge, rightly divide, approve things that are excellent, be sincere without offense, til the day of Christ*

B. The picture is **not** illustrated this way:

Empty self →

← Fill self

C. A more accurate illustration would be this:

↻ Empty Self ↺
Fill Self

It is a cycle of giving up self to Christ and in service to others, then being refilled with God's word and his very Spirit.

In nature, a full body of water becomes stagnant and poisonous if it is not regularly emptied. An empty lake or pond is also useless. It is the cycle of constantly filling and emptying that keeps it fresh and vital.

I. NEED FOR FILLING

Jesus, even though he himself was deity, the Son of God, one with God, found in necessary to have a time to refill, refresh, refuel, renew himself.

A. Pick the phrases that tell of Jesus' need.

Mark 1:35 *solitary place and there He prayed*

Mark 6:31, 32 *come aside by yourselves to a deserted place to re...*

Mark 6:46 *departed to a mountain to pray*

Mark 9:2 *Jesus took Peter, James + John and led them up on a high mountain by themselves*

Mark 14:32 *Sit here while I pray*

B. These glimpses into his communion with God are taken from just one gospel. If you have time, search the other three accounts for similar times.

Luke 22-40-46 -Matt 26-36-44

C. Part of the filling process for us is in gaining **knowledge**.
Study to show thyself approved - to gain "
   1. What warning is found in Hosea 4:6? A similar statement is found in Romans 1:28. *My people are destroyed for lack of knowledge, - Did not like to retain God in their "*
   2. **Knowledge** was an important part of the "wisdom literature." What insight does each of the following verses give?

      Proverbs 2:1-5 *recieve my word, wisdom understanding instruction apply your hearts*

      Proverbs 8:10 *Recieve my knowledge + instruction better than silver + gold.*

      Proverbs 13:16 *prudent man acts with knowledge*

      Proverbs 19:2/Romans 10:2 - *not good for a soul to be without knowledge - have zeal without knowledge*
   3. Where does this knowledge begin (Proverbs 1:7)? *fear of the Lord (Love, Respect, Desire Knowledge)*
   4. Do you regularly fill yourself with knowledge? How do you accomplish this? *By study, attending worship by using the word exercising Wisdom + Understanding*

D. Another part of the filling process is **praise**. By this avenue, our relationship to God becomes more clear. He is recognized as supreme, glorious, magnificent, lord, king, judge, creator, sustainer, all powerful, complete knowledge, and perfect love. Praise is awkward for many because it has not become a habit.

   1. Spend some time reading the last six Psalms (145-150). These are exciting examples of praise.
   Did this, wonderful words
   2. Select one of the above Psalms and write a similar paragraph of praise in your own words. *The Lord is merciful, He is slow to get angry and great is His mercy and compassion. He is good to all. All His being shall please you O Lord. Those who are believers shall glorify + praise you and teach of your power, His kingdom is everlasting He upholds*

Ps 145

all that fall + those who are bowed down. He is righteous in His ways. He is always near to those who call on Him in truth. He will save them + preserves them. all saints shall bless His holy

E. Also part of the filling process is prayer. Our God has opened the doorway to his throne through Christ. He wants us to bring all our needs to him.

1. What is the privilege given in Philippians 4:6? *To require with thanksgiving and prayer needs not wants*
2. In James 5:13 and 16? *pray for the suffering be cheer with those who are, pray for the sick to be healed in the name of Jesus Christ*

III. NEED FOR EMPTYING

Once you have begun to fill the emptiness in your life, the natural result is an outpouring of that in service to others. Again, Christ is the perfect model for us. He gave himself even before Calvary.

A. Notice how much he gave in just a few chapters of Mark.

3:7 — *withdrew Himself with His disciples*

3:20 — *no time to eat*

4:1 — *Teach the multitude on the boat*

5:21 — *Taught the multitude upon crossing the sea*

5:24 — *multitudes followed Him + thronged Him*

6:31 — *look after His disciples*

10:1 — *As He was accustomed He taught the multitudes again in Judea by Jordan*

B. A summary of this principle in his life is found in Mark 10:45. What is it? *To die for sinners, to serve them, not to be served*

Generous Spirit active

C. He illustrated this teaching by parables and by example. What is the point of the parable found in Luke 10:25-37? *To be merciful to others, to love others, to give self*

D. Jesus' most dedicated followers had trouble applying this teaching. In what vivid way did he impress them (John 13:2-7)? *By washing the feet of His disciples, teaching them humility and humbleness*

E. What were their reactions? Peter objected then misunderstanding the purpose ask to be bathed all over

F. How did he sum up his lesson (verses 15-17?) Follow His example, He is just a servant altho He was greater sent from God.

IV. GOD'S PROMISE TO FILL THE EMPTY

A. What blessing is pronounced on those who recognize their hunger (Matthew 5:6)? If we hunger + thirst after righteousness we will be filled

B. How does he fill us? He blesses us with His DBR and His words and examples

Ephesians 5:18 He fills us with His Spirit through His Word

Ephesians 3:19 Be filled with all the fullness of God & His love

John 14:16, 17 He will give us another Helper (HS) to dwell with us and in us.

I Corinthians 3:16 you are the temple of God & that the Spirit of God dwells in you

C. How does one allow himself to be filled (Galatians 2:20)? How is he filled? to be crucified with Christ (DBR) a new creature, old man dead, to live by faith in the Son of God.

D. How do we know this has happened (I John 3:24)?

We keep His commandments We are influenced by the Holy Spirit who He has given us.

CHAPTER 7

WHY AM I TOO BUSY?

CHAPTER 7

... TOO BUSY?

For Christian women, most choices are not between good and evil, but between good, better and best. Deciding the best usage of time and energies and resources when there are so many worthwhile causes, even critical needs, calling for attention, is often overwhelming to the person who is sincerely trying to serve God through serving others.

How can one keep from drowning in activities? What should be left undone? Where do the family and household requirements fit into priorities? Is one shirking Christian responsibilities when these hard choices must be made?

I. **JESUS' EXAMPLE**

Jesus also had to make choices in regard to using his time. By looking at what things had priority for him and how he handled those decisions, a woman can find some plans for herself.

A. In each of the following incidents, Jesus was doing something else when a new opportunity arose. Write down the previous activity in the first column and the interruption in the second. In the third column, write the outcome of his decision.

Incident	Activity	Interruption	Outcome
Mk. 1:38-45			
Mk. 2:1-5			
Lk. 7:11-15			
Mk. 10:13-16			

Mt. 9:18-26 _____

Lk. 23, Jn. 19 _____

    B.   He was able to make these decisions because he knew his goal. What was it? (Matthew 20:28 and Luke 19:10)

    C.   He could say at the end of his life he had accomplished his tasks. Read John 17:4. How could he make that statement? Whose standard had he used?

II. GOD'S PRIORITIES FOR TODAY

    A.   *Read Matthew 6:25-34.*

        1.   What should be the first priority? (verse 33)

        2.   What distractions keep one from this priority? (verse 25)

        Women, by necessity, spend a great deal of time on these very things. Think about this: How much time do you spend on shopping for food, preparing, serving, cleaning up? How much time is spent on buying or sewing clothing, washing, mending, dressing, and similar activities?

        This is one area where efficiency must be developed so that there is time for the more important things. These things cannot be neglected as they are a part of living, but they should not be of primary importance either in one's thinking or in one's time expenditure.

        3.   What reassurance did Jesus give regarding these things?

        4.   What two proofs did he give?

B. *Read Luke 10:38-42.*

   1. Describe the scene (use imagination). _____

      _____

      _____

      _____

   2. Who was hospitable? (verse 38)

   3. What was Mary doing?

   4. Have you ever felt like Martha? (verse 40)

   5. How did Jesus respond? Why? Do you think he was unappreciative of her service?

   6. Can you see a way for Martha to have served Jesus and also have followed Mary's example?

C. *Read Proverbs 31:10-31.*

   This is a description of the "perfect" (or ideal) woman that a mother wanted her son to use as a standard when he chose a wife. (Wouldn't every woman like to have this kind of daughter-in-law?) It also is God's concept of the ideal woman because he included it in his word for us. Does this passage make you feel inadequate? That is not the purpose for it, although it can have that effect. Rather it is a goal for every woman to reach toward and a standard for every young man to use in looking for a wife.

   1. List all the kinds of activities which she does (give verse numbers).

2. How was she able to do all of this without becoming "distracted" like Martha?

verse 13:

verse 15:

verse 27:

III. A PLAN OF ACTION

A. *Dedicate your heart to God.*

1. What do the following verses say about dedication?

Matthew 6:33

Matthew 22:36, 37

II Corinthians 8:5

This dedication requires that you learn what God's will for you might be. This can only come by spending time studying his word, talking with him in prayer, and most important, praising him so that you have a proper perspective as to who he is. The praise makes the dedication easier because you can see more clearly the glory of a relationship with him.

B. *Pray for God's wisdom in making choices.*

1. How can wisdom be attained?

James 1:5

I Kings 3:7-10

Ephesians 1:17 and Colossians 1:9-12

C. *Develop a priority list.*

   1. On the left hand of the following chart, number those items listed in order of their importance to you. Add other important items to the list.

   _____ FAMILY   _____

   _____ FRIENDS   _____

   _____ GOD (Worship, study, prayer)   _____

   _____ HOBBY OR RECREATION   _____

   _____ CHURCH FAMILY   _____

   _____ VOLUNTEER WORK (PTA, scouts, etc.)   _____

   _____ HOUSEWORK   _____

   _____ GROOMING (hair, face, body, clothing)   _____

   _____ TEACHING GOOD NEWS   _____

   _____ JOB   _____

   _____ OTHER_____

   _____ _____

   _____ _____

   _____ _____

2. Cover up those numbers and on the right hand side, estimate how many hours each week you spend in each activity (some activities can be done simultaneously so the time can be counted both places).

   a. Does your time investment match your priority?

   b. What can you presently change to make the two columns more compatible? (Some items will vary at different times in your life, so do not compare your list with another.)

D. *Learn to be efficient in discharging physical responsibilities.*

   1. Are you accountable for using time wisely (Ephesians 5:15, 16)? Does the parable of the talents (Matthew 25:14-30) have any application to time?

   2. What happens when responsibilities are neglected (Titus 2:4-6)?

   One woman expressed her philosophy of keeping things done regularly like this, "I'll tell myself it will only take a minute, so I'll do it now." She applies this to bedmaking, cleaning up a mess, writing a note, etc. How different that is from the philosophy that says, "I'll get to that later." The first is efficient, while the second allows for sloppiness, tardiness, procrastination, and confusion.

   3. How can you be more efficient, especially in tending to the physical things?

E. *Allow for God's action in your life.*

   One preacher refers to the time he spends with people who call unexpectedly by phone or in person as "divine interruptions." He knows that his best ministry is often done at these very times when people are open and teachable. How would his ministry be diminished if his schedule were so full that he could not accept these "interruptions"?

   What divine interruptions do you have in your weekly schedule?

F. *Recognize the "stage" of your life.*

Each woman is at a different place in her lifespan. This applies to singleness/marriage/single-again, to childrearing, to career, to maturity, to spiritual growth, to physical abilities, and to financial resources.

    1. What does Ecclesiastes 3:1-8 say about this?

    2. How does this apply to your life now? In the future?

G. *Include God's promises in your planning.*

Write out the following promises.

Philippians 4:13: _____

_____

_____

Ephesians 3:20, 21: _____

_____

_____

Colossians 3:23, 24: _____

_____

_____

CHAPTER 8

WHY AM I SURROUNDED BY CONFLICT?

CHAPTER 8

... SURROUNDED BY CONFLICT?

Conflict is **disheartening** and discouraging. A mother hears her children fussing with one another and wants to cry, "Where is your love? Don't you know families need to stick together against the world?" A man feels pulled both ways by the jealous rivalry of his co-workers. Neighbors begin to take sides over a boundary dispute. A minister sadly holds his head in his palms as he reflects over the bickering in his congregation.

Conflict is **debilitating**. It robs every one involved of energy, creativity, even desire for better things. It erodes plans and the enthusiasm for them. It is a hungry monster that feeds on negative emotions.

Conflict is **devilish**. Satan cannot abide peace and harmony. His purposes are better served by turmoil and strife which leaves humans weak, confused, and vulnerable.

I. SOURCE OF CONFLICT

God is very specific about the causes of conflict. Perhaps, if each one were aware of the petty, selfish source of this major problem, each would see the foolishness of continuing. It is rather embarrassing when one applies the following verses to one's own quarrel.

A. What causes conflict?

James 4:1-3

Proverbs 15:18 (Proverbs 29:22)

Proverbs 13:10

I Timothy 6:3-5

B. Describe how ambition, selfish desires, pride, etc., develop into strife (or conflict).

C. Can Christians avoid all strife (Romans 12:18)?

II. RESULTS OF CONFLICT

A. James indicates that strife is not the best way to accomplish an end. What does he say will happen (4:4-6)?

B. Paul's fear for the Corinthian church was that he would find it full of conflict when he visited (II Corinthians 12:20). Why would this concern him so?

C. How did Paul earlier describe that same church (I Corinthians 3:3, 4)?

D. Think of a time you were involved in a serious conflict.

1. How did you feel physically?

2. How did it affect you emotionally.

3. Did it have any effect on your spiritual life?

4. Were other relationships affected?

Many people feel that no good change comes without strife. Our country was conceived in turmoil, delivered in warfare, and initiated in regional bickering. And we applaud those early efforts. All around the world today, fighting against perceived injustices continues. When situations become intolerable, revolution seems to be the solution.

On a lesser scale, individual differences usually are not resolved until one party revolts against the status quo. It happens in homes, in business, in government, and in interpersonal relationships. Is conflict the only way to bring about change, or is there a better way?

Conflict may be the easiest, quickest way to force an issue, but it is not necessarily the best. Improvements can be made through peaceful channels, but that way takes more time, more thought, more patience, more selflessness, and more effort. Most people, even Christians, have not been trained to look for and develop peaceful confrontations.

III. WAYS TO LESSEN CONFLICT

A. *Tolerate differences.*

God created differences (in personality, in abilities, in interests) in order to make a complete body. Scan Romans 14:1 - 15:7.

1. From the following verses, find the steps Paul outlines to keep unity.

   14:1

   14:13

   14:19

   15:1

   15:7

2. What is said in II Timothy 2:14 and Romans 14:1 about petty conflicts?

B. *Refrain from talking too much.*

Many quarrels are started by a busybody—someone talking about an issue that in no way relates to him.

1. How is this action described in Proverbs 26:17?

   In Proverbs 17:9?

2. James warns against speaking too quickly. What does he say about this in 1:19, 20 and 1:26?

C. *Don't be the initiator.*

1. Read Proverbs 17:14. Why is it dangerous to start a quarrel?

2. How does one's tone and manner affect a potential quarrel (Proverbs 15:1)?

3. Who should be the one to "right the wrong" done to you (Romans 12:19-21)?

B. *Forgive first and last.*

Forgiveness wets the embers of a flaming conflict. Forgiveness is never easy, but always rewarding. It is especially hard when the other person does not ask for or deserve it. Neither did we ask for or deserve it when Christ died for our sins.

1. Read Romans 5:8. When did Christ die for you?

2. In what way should this motivate you regarding conflict (Ephesians 4:31, 32 and Colossians 3:13)?

E. *Be a peacemaker.*

1. What blessing does Jesus pronounce on peacemakers (Matthew 5:9)?

2. How can a person be a peacemaker? Give specific suggestions.

F. *Learn to love.*

There is a vivid contrast in the way people respond to a lack of love and to the highest love.

1. How is this described in Proverbs 10:12?

2. What importance did Jesus place on this love (Matthew 22:37-40)?

3. What characterizes this love (I Corinthians 13:4-7)?

4. What would this love have to do with conflict? Think about this question; then write as many applications as you can make.

G. *The World and Conflict*

In this imperfect world, even perfect Jesus had conflict. The early Corinthian church, as seen earlier in this study, was full of conflict. Other early groups struggled with the same issues. However, throughout scripture, warnings are given and godly people are encouraged to avoid this destructive force whenever possible.

1. What is the balance (Romans 12:18)?

2. In your world presently, in what aspects of your life do you find yourself embroiled in or surrounded by conflict?

3. What is your responsibility as a Christian in the above conflicts?

4. Based on this lesson, when you cannot avoid a conflict, what should be your attitude?

CHAPTER 9

WHY AM I OFF BALANCE?

CHAPTER 9

... OFF BALANCE?

Religion has earned the reputation of being a laughable exercise in superstition. This has come about through the actions of people who have not heeded God's teaching about balance.

How does one display an attitude of devotion without being fanatical? Does strict adherence to God's word make one a freak in society? How are the paradoxes of the Bible implemented?

Balance is a thread running throughout the Bible. Many "church fusses" are over an insistence upon an extreme stand not taught by Jesus or his followers.

A balanced life gives peace to the Christian and is appealing to those who do not know Christ, even drawing them to him.

I. FINDING SOLID GROUND

In order to stay balanced one must find the solid, safe paths of God.

A. What picture does Christ present of someone who has not built on a solid foundation (Matthew 7:24-26)?

B. What is the foundation that gives balance (I Corinthians 3:11)?

C. Many of the Proverbs teach about instability and wavering. What warning is given in Proverbs 4:26, 27)?

D. In Proverbs 25:28 to what is an unstable person compared?

What "walls" in a person's life become broken by lack of self-control?

E. According to Ecclesiastes 7:18, what should a person avoid?

F. Now read verses 14-17. What are some of the extremes mentioned?

II. AVOIDING EXTREMES

In the following verses, discover the contrasting extremes, either mentioned or implied. Then answer the questions.

A. Ephesians 6:4. Extremes: _____

_____

How can the extremes be avoided in childrearing?

B. I Timothy 2:9, 10. Extremes: _____

_____

Does overdress and underdress equally distract from the Christian life? How?

What is the better "adornment"?

C. Proverbs 30:8, 9. Extremes: _____

_____

What is the danger of each extreme?

Does this request strike a response in your heart? Why?

What does Paul teach about the extreme desire for money (I Timothy 6:6-10)?

What is a balanced attitude toward money?

D. I Corinthians 7:5 (to understand the context, read verses 2-7)

Extremes: _____

_____

What problems evolve if this warning is not obeyed?

Was Paul in tune with human nature? In what way?

E. I Peter 2:16. Extremes: _____

_____

What is the proper balance?

III. BEAUTY OF BALANCE

Jesus scathingly denounced the Pharisees for their lack of balance, calling that particular form of imbalance "hypocrisy." Read Matthew 23:23-28.

A. Where were the Pharisees giving emphasis?

B. What were they neglecting?

C. Which did Jesus say should have been done?

D. What two comparisons did he make to show them the folly?

E. Do you see the same kinds of imbalance in the church today? in your own life? Give specifics.

F. I Thessalonians 5:12-22 is a beautiful description of a balanced Christian life. What things are mentioned?

G. The qualifications for elders include several traits which show a balanced life. From I Timothy 3:2-7 and Titus 1:6-9, which phrases indicate a need for balance?

IV. THE BALANCING ACT

    A.   What areas of your life do you find out of balance?

           What steps can you take to recover balance in those areas?

    B.   Read and memorize II Timothy 1:7. Does this passage give you hope in your ability to strike a balance?

CHAPTER 10

WHY AM I AFRAID TO BE MYSELF?

CHAPTER 10

... AFRAID TO BE MYSELF?

I. **WHO ARE YOU? YOUR IDENTITY.**

What is the first response that came to your mind as you read that question?

It is so easy to lose your identity among the demands of others. As you age from infancy on toward old age, labels are applied to you by other people. You are first child, then sibling, friend, spouse, parent, grandparent, employee, perhaps Christian, maybe boss. You are defined by the kind of work you do. You are limited by perceptions of yourself and others as to what you can become.

Christ gives the only identity necessary. His labels are true and unlimiting.

Sometimes it becomes necessary to take a look at the labels one has accepted as part of his identity and to compare them to the true label from Christ.

It also may be necessary to break the limitations that one has accepted. Are these limits from Christ or from some other source that has no validity in the Christian life?

In this chapter, you will take a look at who you think you are compared to who Christ wants you to be. You will also learn to accept yourself.

II. **YOUR DESCRIPTION OF YOURSELF.**

A. Describe yourself:

1. Physically

2. Mentally

3. Emotionally

4. Socially

5. Spiritually

III. SOMEONE ELSE'S DESCRIPTION OF YOU

A. Find someone who loves you and have that person describe you:

1. Physically

2. Mentally

3. Emotionally

4. Socially

5. Spiritually

B. Do the two descriptions match?

1. In what ways are they different?

2. Why do you think there are differences in the descriptions?

3. Which one is more nearly accurate and why?

IV. YOUR DESCRIPTION OF YOUR HERITAGE

A. Using the chart on the following page, fill in as many spaces as you can.

B. Beside each name that you filled in, write one quality that you received from that person (i.e.: color of hair, love of music, temper, etc.).

C. Answer the following questions.

1. Do you feel good about your heritage?

2. Were most of the qualities possible obtained from that heritage positive or negative?

3. What would you like to change about your heritage?

4. What can you change about your heritage? How?

5. Has knowing Christ affected any other aspect of your heritage? In what way?

V. YOUR ROLE AS A PRINCESS

Regardless of where, to whom, and when you are born, you can be a princess. (If you have already accepted Christ, you are a princess.)

A. What has made (or can make) you a princess (John 1:11-13)?

B. What promise has God given you?

Romans 8:14, 15

II Corinthians 6:18

C. How does an earthly princess act? (Discuss her dress, manners, behavior, children, etc.)

D. What are her privileges?

E. What are her responsibilities?

F. How do these same qualities (from questions 10, 11, 12) apply to daughters of the heavenly king?

VI. YOUR UNIQUENESS

   A. Uniqueness is a beautiful gift. Differences are a cause for celebration. Read I Corinthians 12:12-27.

   B. What general example does Paul use to demonstrate this principle?

      1. What specific examples?

      2. How does this apply to you personally?

   C. Name your favorite:

   Person _____

   Food _____

   Beverage _____

   Teacher _____

   Clothing _____

   Room in your house _____

   Color _____

   Song _____

   Movie _____

   Tree _____

   Flower _____

   State _____

   TV Program _____

   Animal _____

Smell _____

Memory _____

Time of Day _____

Present _____

Bible Character _____

Bible Verse _____

Book in Old Testament _____

Book in New Testament _____

D. Describe:

A perfect day _____

Your ideal self _____

What you want to be doing five years from now _____

_____

What you want to be doing twenty years from now _____

_____

The person you most admire _____

All of these things are what make you special. It is good to have your own dreams, favorites, goals. Don't compare your life, your family, your interests, your accomplishments with anyone else. You are unique.

VII. HOW GOD MAY USE THE UNIQUE YOU

A. *Adequacy of your abilities.*

God will supply all you need, both physically and spiritually. He will make you adequate for the role he has given you.

What promise is found in Philippians 4:19?

In II Corinthians 9:6?

In Ephesians 3:20, 21?

B. *Assessment of your abilities.*

1. List five talents God has given you.

    a. _____

    b. _____

    c. _____

    d. _____

    e. _____

2. List five areas that others do much better than you.

    a. _____

    b. _____

    c. _____

    d. _____

    e. _____

3. How can you presently use your talents most effectively?

4. Do you need to work at developing any of the areas of weakness in question B-2?

5. What areas of weakness should you just forget about and let others supply the ability?

II. THE TIME FOR USING YOUR ABILITIES.

God not only provides the abilities to you, he also sets the timing for you to use those abilities. There is a time for everything God wants you to accomplish in your life.

A. Read Ecclesiastes 3:1-14.

1. List the contrasts. _____

2. Are all of those things accomplished at the same time?

B. God will supply the wisdom you need to find and to accomplish your role in life.

1. Write James 1:5. Memorize it. _____

2. After praying for that wisdom, trust the judgment and insight God gives you. What does James say about believing you will receive it (1:6-8)?

CHAPTER 11

WHY AM I FORGOTTEN?

CHAPTER 11

... FORGOTTEN?

In most cultures, the elderly are revered and honored. Among the Kung Bushmen, the father and mother receive respect and the father is head of his household as long as he lives. The Bedouin young men are expected to defer to the older generation at all times. Throughout the Orient, it is a disgrace to neglect a parent. Lin Yutang, a Chinese philosopher wrote, "How can one be thought wise unless one is thought to be old?" On and on such a listing could go. It is only in the Western world that youth is worshipped and age avoided or disguised.

This lesson is to help people on both sides of the magic elusive age that separates old from young to understand the senior years. For many people, one-fourth of life is after retirement. Twenty percent of the church's membership is in the senior class. When a segment of the family is that large, it must not be neglected or wasted.

I. PROBLEMS AND BENEFITS OF AGING

Complete the following chart.

Problems of aging	Benefits of aging

II. GOD'S VIEW

God's views of time and aging are much different from those of current Western culture.

A. What is His view?

   Proverbs 16:31

   Proverbs 20:29

   Psalm 92:14

B. Solomon describes old age in rather discouraging terms in Ecclesiastes 12:1-7. See if you can match the descriptive phrases to body parts.

   _____

   _____

   _____

   _____

C. Is this a complete picture of aging?

D. Compare the description in Ecclesiastes with Isaiah 40:29-31.

E. Ponder the inward renewal described in II Corinthians 4:16-18.

   This inward renewal is the great beauty of age. Those who allow God to work in their lives radiate his presence even more gloriously as years pass.

III. GOD'S USE OF THE ELDERLY

Moses, Jeremiah and others complained to God that they did not have enough experience for the tasks he assigned them because of their relative youth (Exodus 4 and Jeremiah 1). However, I do not know of a time when anyone tried to excuse himself from service to God because of old age.

A. Make a list of things elderly people can do in spite of health problems, financial restrictions, and limited mobility.

_____

_____

_____

_____

B. Compare your list with what someone is a different age category has written. Discuss the difference in the two lists, each trying to understand the other.

C. What specific task did Paul give older women (Titus 2:3-5)?

What are ways this can be done?

IV. EXAMPLES OF SERVICE BY THE ELDERLY

A. Service at any age can be quite creative. In fact, the more imaginative services are often the most effective. Following are some true stories of service.

1. In a West Texas town lived a lady who because of arthritis was totally bedfast. In her healthier years she had begun a pre-kindergarten. As she lost her mobility, she continued her school. Always there was a waiting list of students. They loved her, her teaching, and her spirit. They helped by fetching things. This woman rarely ever needed her caregiver in the schoolroom. She gave far more to those children than do many young healthy teachers.

2. In Memphis, Tennessee, a housebound elderly Christian woman spread her service across the United States and into other nations. She regularly corresponded with preachers, missionaries, church leaders. She would find someone's name in one of the many church bulletins she received and write an encouraging note. In this way she began many lively correspondences.

3. In Houston, Texas, one man, near 80, is always first to arrive at the church building on Sunday morning. Because of this, he now has the responsibility for unlocking the building which is a great help to the deacon who oversees that function.

4. One of the great encouragers of my life was a sweet Christian woman who, when I first began teaching women, would come every class I taught. I felt inadequate when she was present because I thought (knew) she had so much to offer than I did. She was always encouraging, saying just the right words to keep me trying to improve.

5. In Lubbock, Texas, is an active group of widows who fellowship together regularly. Jokes are made that those who are not widows are jealous of fun these widows enjoy. Their service to one another is tremendous and a very real help to recent widows whom they surround with love and care.

B. Add your own stories of service you have seen by a senior Christian.

C. The list of productive senior citizens from both Bible times and modern history is endless. What great accomplishments have been completed by those wonderful servants.

Who are some Bible characters who served into old age?

V. COOPERATION BETWEEN THE "YOUNG" AND THE "ELDERLY"

Paul understood mutual responsibility. Nowhere is this needed more than between generations.

A. What does he long for in Romans 1:11, 12 and why?

B. Below make a list of things the younger members can do to support and encourage the elderly.

_____

_____

_____

_____

C. Again, compare your list with someone of another generation.

D. Satisfying, productive later years must be planned. What steps can younger people take to assure this in their lives?

VI. GOD'S CONTINUING CARE FOR THE ELDERLY

God continues to have a plan for your life. What comfort is there in Isaiah 46:4?

On his 81st birthday. John Quincy Adams is reported to have answered the question, "How is John Quincy Adams today?" with the following reply:

"John Adams is quite well, thank you. Of course, the house in which he lives is a bit dilapidated. Time and the seasons have nearly destroyed it. It is tottering on its foundations and the roof is worn quite thin. Yes, the old tenement is becoming quite uninhabitable and I fear John Quincy Adams will have to move out of it quite soon. But, he himself is quite well, thank you, quite well."

CHAPTER 12

WHY AM I SO HOMESICK?

CHAPTER 12

... HOMESICK?

A young woman left home to attend college in a distant state. This was something she had long wanted to do. It was exciting and full of promise. But, alas, she soon realized something was missing. She was homesick! It was not a mild fleeting emotion, or even a temporary "down" that would be gone in the morning. She was so emotionally homesick that she was physically ill. As time passed, she learned to live with the "ailment," and it even lessened in intensity. As long as she remembered that her separation from home was only temporary, she was able to keep herself from being overwhelmed. But the feeling was always there. It was not "cured" until her first trip home a few months later.

This is an apt comparison to the feeling Christians have in yearning for that glorious homecoming awaiting them. This temporary sojourn may have some pleasures, but it also has a share of troubles. The real relief, joy, security, and peace will come when they finally travel home.

I. **WHERE IS HOME?**

Why is there such a longing for another place? Because "belonging" is important and Christians do not belong in this world.

    A.   Where is the Christian's citizenship (Philippians 3:20, 21)?

        Who awaits them?

    B.   What makes one a citizen of that land (Romans 8:13-17)?

C. What rights does one have as a citizen there?

   Mark 3:31-35

   II Corinthians 6:18

   Hebrews 2:11

D. Is the present a temporary sojourn (I Corinthians 7:29-31)?

II. WHAT IS THE FATHER'S HOUSE LIKE?

Jesus often talked of the home awaiting him. He also said he would share it with his followers.

A. On what scale is this home to be prepared (John 14:1-4)?

B. Why did Jesus tell his followers about this home?

C. With what materials will this house be furnished (Matthew 6:19-21)?

D. How is this home described (Revelation 21:1-5; 21:22-27; 22:1-6)?

E. What kind of body will the citizens have (I Corinthians 15:35-54 - especially notice 42-44)?

III. DO WE YEARN FOR THE "HOUSE NOT MADE WITH HANDS"?

A. Read II Corinthians 5:1-10.

   1. How does Paul describe the nature of our earthly experience? (verses 1-4)?

   2. How does he contrast the permanent heavenly home (verses 1-4)?

   3. Why did God make us (verse 5) and what guarantee does he give?

4. What confidence did Paul have and how did that affect his desires and goal (verses 6-10)?

B. Read II Peter 3:8-14

1. Peter declares that the Lord is not as slow as some people were saying. What reason does Peter give for the delay (verse 9)?

2. If you are looking toward a home in heaven, what kind of person should you be (verses 11 and 14)?

3. What attitude do those whose home is in heaven have toward that time (verses 12, 13)?

C. Some Christians express a desire for the end of time to come immediately (as did Peter), but others are glad for delay or even have mixed feelings.

1. What are some reasons some welcome delay?

2. Why are others anxious for an immediate return of Christ?

3. Which way do you feel and why?

4. What was Paul's dilemma (Philippians 1:21-24)?

III. IN WHAT WAYS IS HOME BETTER?

A. Compare the present with the real home.

Romans 8:18

II Corinthians 4:17

Ephesians 1:18

B. Read the invitation to come home in Revelation 22:17. How does this make you feel?

CHAPTER 13

WHY AM I UNCERTAIN?

CHAPTER 13

... UNCERTAIN?

Faith can waver, or falter, or fail. It happens to everyone at various times. It is a problem in the church today. It was an even greater problem in the early church. Their world had been turned upside down by belief in the unbelievable, that is, in Christ and all he claimed. They were persecuted and ridiculed. The world conspired to destroy the slightest glimmer of faith.

It is not much different today. Although the persecution is not as harsh or open, subtle pressure and open ridicule are powerful weapons and are used against faithful believers constantly.

John wrote a powerful treatise to defend the basis for faith and to give hope and reassurance to those who falter in faith. This lesson will be based on I John. Read the entire letter carefully and thoughtfully, noting the way John proves the validity of having faith and the assurance he gives to Christians. Then, study the lesson.

I. **JOHN'S AUTHORITY AND ASSURANCE**

What testimony does he give about his right to defend faith and why does he offer it (1:1-3)?

II. **ASSURANCES THROUGH KNOWLEDGE OF THE DEITY**

A. John assumed they knew something. What did he specify in 2:13-14?

B. He says that they could also discern the difference between a teacher with the Spirit of God and an imposter. How (4:2,3)?

C. Along with discerning the spirits, John tells how to distinguish the children of each. What test does he recommend (3:10)?

- D. What keeps the children of God from being led astray (2:26,27)?

- E. What keeps the world from recognizing the children of God (3:1)?

- F. What proves that one has come to know Christ (2:3-5)?

III. **MORE ASSURANCES BASED ON KNOWLEDGE**

Once a firm faith, based on the deity of God, Christ, and the Spirit of God, is established, other assurances come as a result.

- A. What assurance regarding truth do believers have (2:20,21)?

- B. Are you ever confused about what the truth is?

- C. Does realizing you can know the truth help you in your Christian walk? How?

IV. **ASSURANCE OF CONFIDENCE IN APPROACHING GOD**

- A. What is promised to the children of God (5:14,15)?

- B. Do you sometimes feel that this has not been true in your life?

    Give example.

- C. What might make it seem as if God had not given what you asked?

- D. Do you believe this promise (verses 14, 15) is true?

V. ASSURANCE IN CHRIST'S GIFT OF LOVE AND TRUTH

A. *True love is one great gift Christ brought.* John gives assurance about the knowledge and application of that love in the lives of Christians.

1. What knowledge does John describe in 3:16?

2. How do you know what love is (3:16 and 4:9,10)?

3. What results does that produce in the Christian (4:11,12)?

4. How do you know when you belong to the truth (3:18,19)?

5. What shows that you have passed from life into death (3:14,15 and 4:7,8)?

6. To complete the circle, how do you know when you love the children of God (5:2-4)?

7. What facilitates this obedience (verse 4)?

8. How are we assured of God's presence in us (3:24 and 4:13-16)?

VI. FINAL ASSURANCES

One of the greatest areas of concern for many Christians is their final relationship to God and what will happen to them eternally. Some cannot bring themselves to believe that eternal life can be counted on, that they can be sure of attaining it. John is very plain in his statement regarding this. It is the purpose of his letter.

A. Write 5:13. _____

_____

_____

_____

_____

_____

What does this verse mean?

B. As a summary, John lists some final assurances. Find them in 5:18-21.

C. Are you able to believe that you can know all these things John has written?

D. What ones are you finding difficult to fully believe?

E. Does rereading this letter help you with your faith?

A BLESSING

Dear Wonderful Father,

You are our God. Your glory encompasses, your power overwhelms; and your love sustains. Thank you for your care and provision.

May each person who studies your word be blessed and changed. Bless the study of the subjects in this book.

Each of your children is unique and only you can understand and answer the questions and circumstances of each. May your people ever search for your will in all life situations.

It is because of the unselfish gift of your son that we can ask these things.

Amen